Tracy

Costume in Context
The Victorians

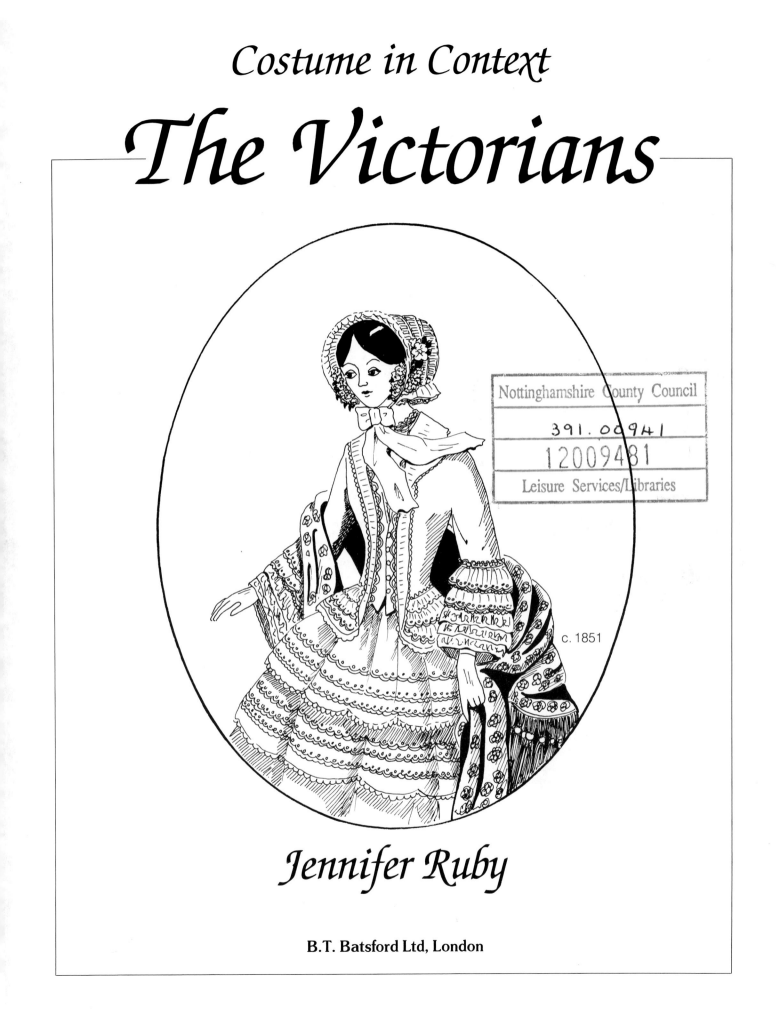

c. 1851

Jennifer Ruby

B.T. Batsford Ltd, London

Foreword

When studying costume, it is important to understand the difference between fashion and costume. Fashion tends to predict the future – that is, what people *will* be wearing – and very fashionable clothes are usually worn only by people wealthy enough to afford them. For example, even today, the clothes that appear in fashionable magazines are not the same as those being worn by the majority of people in the street. Costume, on the other hand, represents what people are actually wearing at a given time, which may be quite different from what is termed 'fashionable' for their day.

Each book in this series is built round a fictitious family. By following the various members, sometimes over several generations – and the people with whom they come into contact – you will be able to see the major fashion developments of the period and compare the clothing and lifestyles of people from all walks of life. You will meet servants, soldiers, street-sellers and beggars as well as the very wealthy, and you will see how their different clothing reflects their particular occupations and circumstances.

Major social changes are mentioned in each period and you will see how clothing is adapted as people's needs and attitudes change. The date list will help you to understand more fully how historical events affect the clothes that people wear.

Many of the drawings in these books have been taken from contemporary paintings. During the course of your work perhaps you could visit some museums and art galleries yourself in order to learn more about the costumes of the period you are studying from the artists who painted at that time.

This book is for Shirley, who encouraged me through all the difficult times, and because she is now 'quite cold with interest'.

Acknowledgments

My thanks to Margaret and Vernon Smith of the Beresford House Museum of Costume in Alresford, Hampshire, for their kindness and for allowing me free access to their fascinating costume collection on numerous occasions.

A large amount of information has been taken from contemporary paintings, in particular: page 16, 'The Poor Teacher' by Richard Redgrave; page 17, 'A Portrait of his Little Daughter' by James Hayllar; page 40, 'The Old Housekeeper', portrait by Henry Stacey Marks; page 44, 'The Squire and the Gamekeeper' by James Lobley; page 60, 'Derby Day 1858' by William Powell Frith. The colour drawing of the pink ball dress is after 'The Reception' by James Tissot, and the market scene is after 'Market Day' by Glendinning.

© Jennifer Ruby 1987
First published 1987

Typeset by Tek-Art Ltd, Kent
and printed in Great Britain by
R J Acford, Chichester, Sussex
for the publishers
B.T. Batsford Ltd
4 Fitzhardinge Street
London W1H 0AH

ISBN 0 7134 5473 3

Contents

Date List

1837	Queen Victoria comes to the throne.
1840	Railways are being built all over Britain and trade is increasing.
1851	Prince Albert organizes the Great Exhibition in Hyde Park. The design of the crinoline (1856) is similar to the Crystal Palace in which the exhibition is held.
1851	Isaac Singer, an American inventor, patents the sewing machine. It does not catch on in Britain until the 1870s.
1854-6	The Crimean War is fought by Britain and France against Russia. Florence Nightingale begins her life's work for hospitals.
1856	Fast dyes for printing all types of material are introduced. Called aniline dyes, they are developed from coal tar.
1861	The death of Prince Albert. Queen Victoria enters a long period of mourning and seclusion. From this there develops a fashion amongst the middle classes for the wearing of black for at least one year after the death of a loved one.
1863	One of the first department stores is opened by William Whiteley in Westbourne Grove, London.
1863	London's underground railway is opened.
1869	The 'boneshaker' bicycle appears.
1870	The Education Act, making it compulsory for children to attend school.
1876	Bell's telephone invented in the U.S.A.
1878	The first public telephone exchange in London.
1885	The first motor car in Germany.
1890s	Penny Bazaars are opened in Manchester by Michael Marks. Goods are sold very much more cheaply at these bazaars as they are bought by self selection and because there is a fast turnover. This means that fashionable lace and trimmings can be bought by greater numbers of women who have not been able to afford them previously.
1890s	Women are beginning their fight for emancipation.
1901	Death of Queen Victoria.

Introduction

The reign of Queen Victoria was a long one and saw many changes which profoundly influenced styles of dress. The industrial expansion of the nineteenth century meant that cities were grimy and smoky and, therefore, men tended to wear darker, more practical colours than in previous years. In contrast, women wore brightly coloured and highly decorated dresses which, in part, reflected the technical improvements in the textile industry. For example, fast dyes for printing all types of material were introduced in 1856 and were instantly successful, and the invention of the sewing machine, although slow to catch on in England, gave greater scope to dress-makers, and fashions gradually became more and more elaborate.

As trade increased both at home and abroad, a greater variety of materials were available. These included Macclesfield silk, lightweight wools such as cashmere, fine linen from Ireland and printed cottons. Specialist wool yarns were imported along with fine silks from France and the Far East. Both hand-made and machine-made lace were popular for trimming and for accessories. Sometimes this lace originated in England, such as the famous Honiton lace, but often it was imported from France and Belgium.

morning dress, silk taffeta, c. 1860

During the second half of the century many more shops were springing up in the expanding towns and cities, selling items such as lace, ribbons and satins which had been mass produced. This meant that more women could afford the fashionable frills and flounces of the time as they could buy their own trimmings and add them themselves to their dresses. Poorer folk, however, had to be content with gazing into the shop windows.

The development of the railway network in Britain was also important as it increased communications and added to the speed at which goods could be transported from the factories to shops, thus making the whole manufacturing industry more efficient. The railways also added their share of grime and soot to the atmosphere and you can imagine that many of the dresses worn by the fine ladies of the time would have become extremely dirty, especially as many of the fabrics could not be washed and there were no dry cleaners at that time!

The growth of the manufacturing industry also saw the rise of the 'self-made' man, and many men, rather than inheriting wealth and social status, became rich through hard work and shrewd business practice. They were then able to buy luxuries for themselves and their families, which included fine and extravagant clothes that would have been undreamed of in their fathers' day. There was still a huge gap between the rich and the poor, however, and you may find it interesting to compare the clothes of different people in society. For example, the fine dresses worn by fashionable ladies were very different from the garments worn by their dressmakers, who sweated many hours for low wages in order to please their customers, and the fashions in the wardrobe of a rich manufacturer's wife would be a far cry from the state-owned clothes handed out to the women in the workhouse.

It is also interesting to look at how the shape of fashions altered during Queen Victoria's reign, and you might like to consider why some of these changes occurred. For example, in 1851 the Great Exhibition in London displayed with pride Britain's achievements in art and industry. The exhibition was held in the newly constructed Crystal Palace. The shape of the crinoline petticoat which appeared in 1856 in fact bore a remarkable resemblance to the design of the Crystal Palace! It would seem, therefore, as if fashions expanded just as industry expanded, and women displayed their costly dresses with pride just as the nation displayed its technical achievements.

A London street, c. 1851

Towards the end of the century, women were beginning to fight for emancipation and this also affected the shape of fashion. For example, their desire to be equal with men was reflected in the leg-of-mutton sleeves which appeared at the time, giving women a more aggressive and less feminine appearance. In addition, their increased participation in sporting activities saw the beginning of a demand for clothes which would allow more freedom of movement for cycling, swimming or playing golf and tennis.

Finally, in the background, there was Queen Victoria herself, a proud and dignified queen, who was not only the head of a prosperous nation and a huge empire, but also of a large family. In fact, the sense of 'family' and family life was very strong in Victorian times, and whether rich or poor, families lived, worked and played together with a sense of closeness that, to a large extent, has been lost in our own day. In this book you will follow a solicitor's family through the Victorian age. While you are looking at the clothes the members of the family wore, think about the kind of lives they led and compare them with those of some of the other families portrayed in the book.

A London street, c. 1881

A Solicitor in London, c. 1851

In previous centuries it was always accepted that a man's dress in some way reflected his standing in society. For example, a duke would wear rich and extravagant clothes as if proclaiming his noble birth to the world. In Victorian times, however, with the growth of the industrial middle class in England, many more men were able to afford good clothes and it was no longer considered 'good form' for a man to parade his wealth. It was difficult, therefore, to tell the difference between a man who was *born* wealthy and a man who had *made* his wealth, because they were both dressed like gentlemen. In addition, the smoky, grimy and sooty atmosphere created in the towns by the factories and railways seemed to colour men's clothing with a kind of sombre drabness. Darker colours are, of course, more practical in a dirty atmosphere, and were worn by most men.

Here is a solicitor who lives and works in London. He is reasonably affluent and can, therefore, afford to dress himself and his family in fashionable clothes.

He is wearing a double-breasted frock coat in dark olive green, brown trousers, which are narrow in the leg and cover his shoes, a white shirt with a stand-up collar and a fashionably large bow-tie. He is also wearing gloves and carries a cane. He has very curly side whiskers, which are known as 'mutton-chops', and his hair is dressed with oil to keep the style in place.

On the right, you can see some more garments from the solicitor's wardrobe. The shirt is cotton and has two panels of tucks down the front, turn-back cuffs and pearl buttons. It is hand sewn.

The drawers are pink silk stockinette and also have pearl buttons. The six holes that you can see in the waistband are all bound with tape and are for securing his braces.

The waistcoat below is one of many in the solicitor's collection. It is single-breasted, which means that it will be worn under a double-breasted coat like the one on the left. (A double-breasted waistcoat would be worn under a single-breasted coat.) This waistcoat is silk and is heavily embroidered. In fact, waistcoats were one of the few items of clothing that were still colourful in a man's wardrobe.

The solicitor usually wears lace-up shoes or ankle boots, and always has a top hat. Although he is seen in the picture with a cane, he might carry an umbrella instead but is rarely seen without one or the other when out walking.

turn-back cuffs

The Solicitor's Wife, c. 1851

On the right you can see the solicitor's wife, who is always fashionably dressed. Her lilac-coloured dress has a tight-fitting jacket-like bodice which is shaped to the waist and flairs out with two flaps edged with lace. The bodice is open at the bosom and is lined with lace, and she has lace ruffles at the sleeves. The skirt is very full and is supported by a number of petticoats. Her bonnet is also lilac and has a very open shape. It is lined with white satin and trimmed at the sides with tufts of small white and red roses. Her shawl is made of cashmere, which is a fine, soft wool.

You can imagine that it takes a great deal of time and money to create this fashionable look, but this lady has the resources to enable her to wear these beautiful and expensive clothes. In fact, this is only one of many such dresses in her wardrobe.

Underneath her dress she is wearing a chemise and drawers. On top of this are her stays, which are stiffened with whalebone and are very tightly laced in order to give her a tiny waist. Over this she wears a camisole to protect her dress from the stays, and, finally, six petticoats to make the dress stand out and display the richness of the material. You can imagine that all this is rather uncomfortable!

Below is an example of one of her camisoles and two of her caps, which she always wears indoors.

Her wardrobe collection also contains a number of parasols. These were essential for keeping the sun from a lady's face as it was considered most unseemly, and indeed unfortunate, to have a suntan. In the 1850s it was the fashion for parasols to be small. The one pictured here has a hinged handle, which makes it easier to fold up when she gets into her carriage.

All of her shoes are low heeled and very dainty. When she attends a ball with her husband, she wears thin-soled slippers of white satin.

camisole

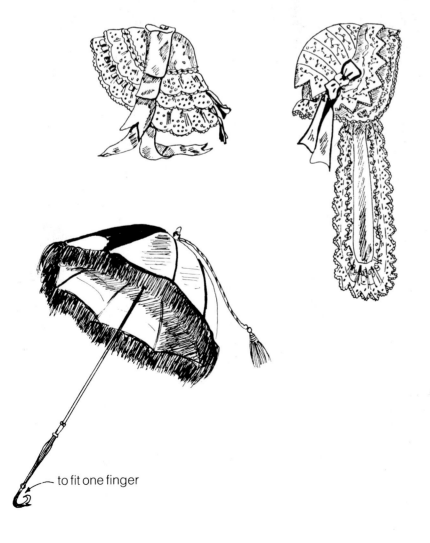

— to fit one finger

The Solicitor's Children, c. 1854

Here are the solicitor's three children: Jane, Emma and Edward. As you can see, it was the custom to dress children as miniature adults, and very little thought was given to their desire and need to be able to play and move freely.

Jane is wearing a dress of green printed taffeta, trimmed with ribbon. It has a tight bodice, short sleeves, and undersleeves made of cambric, which is a fine white linen.

Jane

Emma

Emma is wearing a blue dress with a low collar and bell-shaped sleeves with turn-back cuffs and undersleeves. Like Jane, she has her hair plaited neatly in place, though she has the addition of a large blue ribbon. Both girls are wearing numerous petticoats and they also have on pantalettes (or pantaloons). Pantalettes were similar to drawers, but they were longer, reaching to just below the calf, and they were often trimmed with lace and tucks.

Edward is playing outside with his hoop. As little boys were always dressed as girls until they were about five years old he is wearing what appear to us to be very feminine clothes. His dress is grey and has maroon velvet trimming that matches the trimming on his hat. He has long, curly hair, satin boots with varnished tips and, as he is outside, he is also wearing white kid gloves.

The problem with these clothes was that they were impractical for growing children who, quite naturally, wished to play and romp about. In fact, the frills and flounces were often a fire hazard. Little girls were frequently laced up very tightly into their dresses in order to give them the tiny waist that was fashionable. How healthy do you think this was?

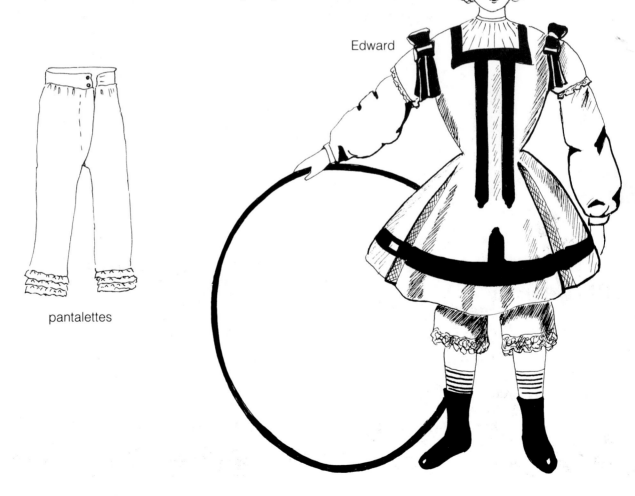

Edward

pantalettes

A Young Maid and Her Sister, c. 1854

This little maid works in the solicitor's house. She is wearing a printed cotton dress. As cotton was becoming cheap and was easy to wash it would have been her usual working attire. She also wears a smart, bibbed white apron and a mob cap under which her hair is carefully concealed. On no account must she allow her curls or ringlets to escape as she must appear smart but not too decorative, and certainly not fashionable!

She is carrying a large copper kettle which is probably very heavy. Her day is a demanding one and involves a great deal of carrying, sweeping, cleaning and endless trips up and down stairs. Occasionally she has even been asked to iron the newspaper before it goes upstairs to the master as he is very particular that his paper does not appear to have been read before he receives it.

Although the work is hard and the hours long, the maid feels that she is quite well off in that she has good food, plenty of company and is receiving a training for marriage. At the moment, she earns £10 a year. Eventually, she hopes to be promoted to housemaid, which will, of course, provide her with more money.

The maid's sister Alice is not so fortunate. She works for a dressmaker, where the conditions are appalling. Several girls work together for long hours in a small, cramped room, stitching the lacy shirts and fine garments worn by people like the solicitor and his family. Alice has her hair tightly bound in a net and is wearing a plaid, close-fitting jacket over a flaired dress with a double flounce. She is paid 3d (1½p) per shirt. Can you imagine how tired her eyes must be?

Although the sewing machine had already been invented in America it was rarely used in England and, besides, many ladies preferred their clothes to be hand sewn. This extract comes from a poem by Thomas Hood which he published anonymously in the magazine *Punch* in 1843. It tells of the plight of seamstresses like Alice who worked so hard to produce the fine, fashionable garments required by the gentry.

Work-work-work
'Til the brain begins to swim;
Work-work-work
'Til the eyes are heavy and dim;
Seam and gusset and band
Band and gusset and seam
'Til over the buttons I fall asleep
And sew them on in my dreams!

Work-work-work
Oh men with mothers and wives,
It is not linen you're wearing out
But human creatures' lives.
Stitch! stitch! stitch!
In poverty hunger and dirt,
Sewing at once with a double thread
A shroud as well as a shirt.

The Governess and Her Sister, c. 1854

This is Anne, the governess to the solicitor's children. Her clothes are modest, partly because she is not wealthy, but also because she must remember her position as a servant. As such she must be prepared to blend into the background and not appear too ostentatious.

She is wearing a plain, dark grey woollen dress and has a piece of linen edged with lace draped around her neck. She looks neat but there are none of the fine frills and flounces that appear on the clothes of the girls she teaches. In a famous novel by Charlotte Brontë, a governess called Jane Eyre also tells of the plain clothes that she must wear while the ladies of the house in which she teaches all wear finery.

Anne is reading a letter which could possibly have come from her parents, who live near Manchester. She has had to travel far from home for her job and lives in with the solicitor's family. She earns £20 per year.

Her sister Margaret is also working in London, though the girls rarely see each other. Margaret is working as a children's nanny in another household and you can see her on the opposite page with one of her charges. She is wearing a plain, black dress with white collar and cuffs and a white apron and cap trimmed with lace.

The girls miss their home and their parents but it has been necessary for them to find work as their father cannot afford to support them. Only certain kinds of jobs were considered 'respectable' for young ladies from 'good' families.

The little girl is getting ready to go out to a party and is wearing her best party dress. It looks rather stiff and uncomfortable as it is supported by several petticoats. Her cloak is bright red and edged with fur. Red party cloaks were very popular with little girls at this time and became almost like a uniform. This was mainly due to the fact that the fairy tale *Little Red Riding Hood* was so well read and liked by Victorian children.

A Country Parson and His Wife, c. 1854

Here are the parents of the governess and her sister who live in a village just outside Manchester. Their father is a country parson and, therefore, does not have a great deal of money. You can see that he wears clothes very similar in style to the solicitor though he does not appear as fashionable and, of course, he wears his clerical collar. His whole outfit is a very dark colour, probably black, due to his profession. He wears a single-breasted frock coat and waistcoat and, like most men at this time, he has a top hat and carries a cane. The parish provides him only with the clothes required for his church services; namely, his preacher's surplice. Even if he were interested in fashion he would not have the money to buy more clothes. In fact, some of his small income is spent on the upkeep of a horse. This is a necessity, for living in a rural area, some of his parishoners live down muddy cart tracks which are not even suitable for a gig.

His wife is dressed in a printed cotton lawn dress which you will notice is much simpler in style and more practical than that of the solicitor's wife. Her shawl is made of wool and is quite plain, and her bonnet, although pretty, is not elaborate. She is carrying a basket which contains a few items for a poor family in the parish. She visits them frequently as the father of the family is ill, from working in the nearby cotton mill, and can, therefore, provide little for his wife and children.

Having little money to spare, the parson's wife frequently makes her own indoor caps and taught her daughters to do the same. The one pictured below is a dress net for her hair which she made by knotting gold thread. It is very intricate and must have taken her many hours to complete.

Can you think of any other reasons why country people, like the parson and his wife, did not dress as fashionably as those who lived in the towns?

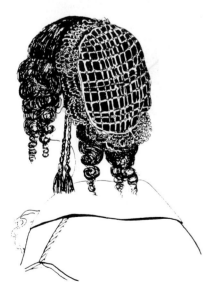

The Owner of a Cotton Mill, c. 1854

This is Mr Brown, the owner of a cotton mill in Manchester. He inherited the factory from his father and has worked hard to build it up and make it profitable. He is very rich but his clothes are not that different from those of the solicitor. Mr Brown sees his work almost like a religion, and money as a tool. He likes to be thrifty and practical, so he dresses like a gentleman but without a great display of wealth. All his money has been earned rather than inherited, and he will use it to buy power and social position.

He is wearing a brown frock coat, dark beige trousers, a white shirt and a bow tie. His waiscoat is the only colourful part of his clothing as it is canary yellow with brown stripes. He has a top hat and a cane, like all gentlemen at this time.

Mr Brown lives close to the mill with his widowed mother. She is a strict and haughty lady who is proud of the achievements of her family. She is always seen dressed in rustling black silk which gives her a very dignified air.

The sombre colours worn by Mr Brown and his mother give them the grave look of authority, yet, living so close to the mill with its continual belching black smoke, their colours are also practical in the grimy sooty atmosphere.

Two Factory Girls, c. 1854

Here are two young girls who work in Mr Brown's cotton factory. It is their dinner hour and they have come outside to enjoy the fresh air and have their lunch. It is a welcome break as they work long hours – sometimes as many as 16 a day.

You will see that their clothes are very simple. They are both wearing white, full-length pinafores over their dresses and have their hair tightly bound in unbecoming hair nets. On their feet they are wearing wooden-soled, leather clogs with a metal rim, which are very ugly indeed when compared to the dainty shoes worn by the ladies of fashion.

This style of dress is, of course, practical for factory work where the conditions are dirty, noisy and sometimes dangerous. For example, in the carding room, where the cotton is combed before it is spun, little bits of fluff fly off from the cotton and fill the air with a white dust. This often makes it difficult to breathe and many employees develop asthma and other diseases of the lungs.

A Soldier, c. 1856

It is now 1856 and we will return to London. This is the young brother of the solicitor who is an officer in the Scots Fusilier Guards. He has been fighting in the Crimean War and has come home to visit his family.

In the early stages of the Crimean War, the soldiers had to fight in the same dress that they wore at home on parade, the only difference being that they were given a cloak and haversack. It does not seem as if it would be very practical to go into battle dressed exactly as if parading in London. What do you think?

On the right you can see that the officer is wearing his cloak rolled over his shoulder to make it easier to carry. His jacket is scarlet with gold buttons and his trousers are a very dark green. It is interesting that many aspects of military uniform are derived from national costumes. For example, the bearskin hat worn by this soldier was originally part of the Turkish national dress.

The solicitor is surprised to see that his brother has a moustache because he thought soldiers had to be clean shaven. The young soldier explains that all ranks in the army have recently been given permission to grow moustaches, so long as they leave at least two inches between the corner of the mouth and the side whisker.

The soldier mentions some of the horrors of the war, and tells the family about Florence Nightingale and how much she has done at Scutari.

A Nurse, c. 1856

Florence Nightingale was really the true founder of modern nursing as we know it today. She lifted the profession of nursing to a new level of respectability. Before she began her work much nursing had been carried out by women from poor, and sometimes unsavoury backgrounds. In fact, it had not been unusual to find a nurse drunk on duty. The soldier explains that when Florence Nightingale went to Scutari to give her help to the casualties of the Crimean War she took with her 38 nurses, most of them nuns from religious orders, and selected the following for their uniform:

A grey tweed dress called a wrapper
A grey worsted jacket
A plain white cap
A short woollen cloak
A holland scarf on which 'Scutari Hospital' was embroidered.

In 1860 Florence Nightingale opened the Nightingale Training School for Nurses at St Thomas's Hospital in London, which at last established an independent career for ladies. On the right you can see one of the nurses from this hospital. She is wearing a brown dress with white collar and cuffs and a snowy white apron and cap. The style of clothing Florence Nightingale chose for her nurses was a cross between that worn by nursing nuns and household servants.

Florence
Nightingale

The Crinoline, c. 1856

In December 1856 the crinoline was invented, and the picture shows the solicitor's wife wearing one under her dress. The crinoline was a hooped cage made of flexible steel or whalebone, and was worn in order to support the wide skirts that were so fashionable. You can imagine that this invention made women feel very free after the suffocation of the layers of petticoats that they had worn in the past. Also, it made them feel important due to the amount of space that they took up with their rapidly expanding skirts!

As the skirts of ladies' dresses were now so wide, it became difficult to wear a full-length coat. This meant that capes, shawls and three-quarter-length coats became fashionable. Below, on the right, the solicitor's wife is wearing a three-quarter-length mantle which is shaped to the waist in front but flows loosely behind in order to accommodate her very full skirt.

fashionable boots

The crinoline also meant that the slightest wind caused the skirt to fly up and expose a pretty ankle. Consequently, boots and shoes now became more elaborate and worthy of being seen by an observant gentleman!

One invention at this time, which proved to be a complete failure, was the inflatable crinoline, which was made of indiarubber tubes instead of metal hoops. It could be blown up to whatever size a lady wished. However, the idea never caught on due to the fact that a few unfortunate ladies experienced punctures! Imagine how embarrassing this would be!

It is an interesting fact that the Victorians had a horror of drowning and many of them liked to have something about their person that would help them to float if necessary. Perhaps the inflatable crinoline would have been useful for this!

inflating a crinoline

The Crinoline Expands, c. 1861

By the 1860s, the popularity of the crinoline had increased greatly and the skirts of fashionable ladies often reached enormous proportions, sometimes measuring as much as 18 feet in circumference! This often caused problems. For example, it became impossible for two ladies to enter a room together or to sit on the same sofa, as their masses of frills and lace took up all the available space!

Here is the solicitor's eldest daughter, Jane, who is all ready for her first ball. She is wearing a very large crinoline under a dress made of three separate materials in colours that tone in with each other. The overskirt is of white gauze; under this is a skirt of yellow satin and, under that, a dark yellow skirt with a black flounce. The dress has been lavishly decorated with ribbons, rouches and flowers.

The width of a lady's skirt at this time was also something of a status symbol. This was because a great amount of material, lace and trimmings would be very expensive, so Jane is showing off her father's wealth with her beautiful dress.

The crinoline, though less exaggerated, was also popular with women in other social classes and, once again, it caused many problems.

Here is the little maid in the solicitor's house, who has now been promoted to parlour maid. Under her black dress she is wearing a hooped petticoat as an artificial crinoline because she cannot afford a real one. But she has just been told by the mistress not to wear one at all because her hoop has been known to sweep a few valuable ornaments off the shelf when she is dusting!

Unfortunately, cheap crinolines had a habit of collapsing in the rain which could be very embarrassing for the wearer.

Perhaps the greatest disadvantage of the crinoline was that it was a fire hazard. Many casualties resulted from crinolines getting set alight and they were forbidden in some factories. Cautaulds textile factory, for example, even imposed fines on girls who wore crinolines to work.

Can you think of any other situations when a crinoline might have been dangerous?

A Ratcatcher and His Wife, c. 1861

Having looked at people closely following fashion, we will now go outside into the streets of London and meet some very different characters. Over the next few pages you will see people whose styles of dress changed very little over the years. Their clothes were chosen for their practicality and availability rather than to meet the demands of fashion.

This is Jack Black, who is the ratcatcher to Queen Victoria. We know this because he wears a sash over his coat, embroidered with a crown and the letters VR, which advertises his profession.

He is proud of his position and his clothes are quite smart. He wears white leather breeches, a great coat (a kind of overcoat) and a scarlet waistcoat. He also has a gold band round his top hat. He tells us: "I make a first-rate appearance, such as is becoming the uniform of the Queen's rat-ketcher."

Other ratcatchers in the city also wore a sash advertising their trade, but you can be sure they were not as well-dressed as Jack Black!

a city ratcatcher

His wife is working in Covent Garden Market. She is wearing very practical clothes, quite different from the crinolines and frills which we have just been looking at.

She has on a striped cotton dress, a woollen shawl and low-heeled shoes. She is carrying her basket of vegetables with the aid of a head-pad, a device used by many of those working in the market. A porter, for example, would wear a supporting pad attached to his hat which was known as a 'porter's knot'. You can see one in the picture below.

Because of lack of money and the need to be practical, many of the women working in Covent Garden would have made their own clothes, and when these became worn and tattered they would repair them. Sometimes, an old skirt could be cut up and made into a garment for a child and then, when that child grew out of it, it could be passed down to a younger brother or sister.

a 'porter's knot'

A Costermonger and His Wife, c. 1861

In another street we meet Dick, the costermonger, who earns his living by selling fresh vegetables from his donkey barrow. He needs clothes that are practical and hard-wearing for his life outside in the dirty city streets.

He wears a small cloth cap a little to one side (he never wears a top hat because he sometimes carries a basket on his head), a dark corduroy waistcoat with brass buttons, a coat of coarse material with large pockets and heavy corduroy trousers.

It was customary for costermongers to wear bright, gaudy neckerchiefs and good strong boots. In fact, it was possible to recognize a costermonger by these two items of clothing.

Dick usually takes his young son with him to help him on his round and, at the same time, learn the trade. The boy is dressed as a smaller version of his father. He is only eight years old and works in the streets from six in the morning until seven at night. Often Dick takes the boy to the local public house after the day's work is over and gives him part of his beer. It is not unusual, therefore, to see the child reeling drunk in the tap room.

Dick's wife is sitting a few streets away selling oranges. She is dressed very simply and probably not warmly enough as it is raining, and you can see that her dilapidated umbrella gives her little protection.

She is wearing a black velveteen bonnet decorated with a few flowers, a thin woollen dress and a cotton apron. Like many other women street-sellers she wears a plaid shawl for a little extra warmth. Underneath her dress she is wearing several cotton petticoats and her footwear is a pair of stout brown boots.

There are no crinolines, parasols or satin slippers in this lady's wardrobe because she does not have the money for them and, besides, the flimsy clothes of fashion would be quite impractical for her.

The Costermonger's Daughter, c. 1861

This is Mary, Dick's ten-year-old daughter. Usually she sell oranges in the streets like her mother but, as oranges are expensive at present, she is selling flowers instead.

She is wearing a faded green cotton dress and a brown apron and she has one of her mother's old shawls draped around her for extra warmth. You will notice that she has no head covering so if she is cold she must put the shawl over her head for protection. Her hair is tangled, matted and dirty and her face and hands are brown from being outside in all weathers. This is in contrast to the daughters of the solicitor, who would never go outside without their bonnets and gloves.

Mary does have sturdy boots, however, even though many street children go barefoot. This is because her father, like many costermongers, is very particular about footwear for himself and his family. Dick would consider it a bitter humiliation if a member of his family did not have good boots and would never allow any of them to wear a pair of second-hand ones, or 'translators', as he calls them.

Lady of fashion, c. 1838

The oyster stall, c. 1851

The hurdy-gurdy player, c. 1851

Gentlemen, c. 1852

Soldier from the Crimean War, c. 1854

Flower seller, c. 1870

Brothers and sisters, c. 1856

Evening dress, c. 1886

Market day, c. 1898

Street Arabs, c. 1861

These young boys are known as street Arabs. They are orphans and spend their days earning money as crossing sweeps. At night they stay in a lodging house run by a costermonger's wife.

Together with some other children they have formed a company of crossing sweeps and mostly work together near Trafalgar Square, sweeping the mud and filth clear for the passing of rich folk who do not wish to dirty their fine clothes.

The boys themselves are dressed in little more than rags and tatters and have no shoes at all. They do not earn very much as sweeps, and they have to buy their own brooms which do not last very long in wet weather. Because of this, the eldest boy often supplements his income by thieving. His outer coat is very thin and made of dark linen. He has purposely torn holes in it in places so that if he picks a pocket he can very quickly put his booty through the holes in his outer coat into the pockets of the one underneath.

You might like to compare the clothes and lifestyle of these children with those of the children you met earlier in the book.

The Workhouse, c. 1861

There were many workhouses in England in Victoria's reign. They were lodging houses which provided food, clothing and shelter for the poor and homeless. The poor only went there as a last resort, however, as conditions inside were often harsh in order to discourage them from remaining. The women were separated from the men, the work was extremely hard and the food was meagre.

This young woman is destitute. She is without a home, a husband or an income and so she is sitting on the steps of the workhouse waiting to be taken in. She is wearing the only clothes she has: a cotton dress, an old shawl and a pair of boots. Her child is wrapped in a blanket. When she enters the workhouse her clothes will be taken from her, she will be searched, ordered to bathe and then she will be issued with a set of clothes.

Each workhouse provided its own style of dress for those lodging within its gates but, generally, it consisted of shapeless, colourless dresses for the women and dingy shirts and ill-fitting trousers for the men. Children had their heads shaved, so that there would be no risk of an epidemic of lice, and were given clothes of coarse woollen material, which were good in winter but, of course, much too hot in the summer.

This is the woman's ward of the workhouse. The lady on the right has only just arrived. She has come with her husband but has been separated from him and will be allowed to see him only once a week. She is wearing her own clothes at present and carries all her possessions in a bundle under her arm. She has been told to begin cleaning as soon as she has changed into her workhouse 'uniform'.

The old ladies in the picture have been in the workhouse for a long time. They are wearing grey woollen dresses, dingy white aprons and caps and brown shawls. The lady in the middle has been sewing coarse material into dresses for new inmates of the workhouse.

Here are a few lines from a poem written by James Reynolds. He had spent some time in Newmarket workhouse in 1846 and, in the poem, he tries to describe his dress:

And now then my clothes I will try to portray;
They're made of coarse cloth and the colour is grey,
My jacket and waistcoat don't fit me at all;
My shirt is too short, or I am too tall;
My shoes are not pairs, though of course I have two,
They are down at the heel and my stockings are blue . . .

Emma's Wedding, c. 1872

We will now move forward to a
spring morning in 1872 and
Emma's wedding day. Jane,
who is already married, is
helping Emma to arrange
her dress before the
church ceremony.

crinolette

The sewing machine was now coming into more general use in England and you can see evidence of it in the abundance of frills and flounces on the dresses of both girls. If you look carefully at the dresses you will also notice how the fashionable shape has altered since the 1860s. The crinoline was no longer in vogue and, instead, ladies wore what was known as a 'bustle'. This was a support which lifted the dress high at the back of the waist. It was usually either a pad or a few hoops of steel or whalebone inserted into the top of a petticoat. Sometimes a bustle, in the form of steel half hoops, would be permanently attached to the top of a crinolette (a half crinoline), as you can see on the right. This had the effect of creating a flat appearance in the front of the dress with all the fullness and bulk of material at the back.

Emma's dress is made of white silk and is decorated with cream trimmings and flowers. Jane's is blue satin with deep blue frills and flounces.

Every bride likes to have a beautiful trousseau when she marries. Emma is no exception and here you can see a few of the items from her wardrobe. She is marrying a young squire who lives in Hampshire and after the wedding she will be moving away from London to his mansion in the country.

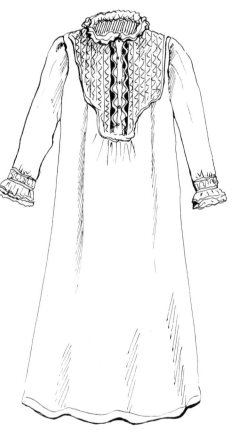

cotton nightdress

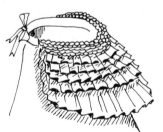

bustle pad

fan

corset

parasol

shoes

The Young Squire, c. 1872

This is the rich young squire who is now Emma's husband. Here you can see him relaxing at home in Hampshire.

He is wearing a fashionable smoking jacket of maroon velvet with a quilted white satin lining. As he is wearing the jacket open, his waistcoat is double-breasted. His trousers are grey tweed and somewhat narrow, and he wears black patent leather shoes.

The squire is very fond of sport and his wardrobe is fully equipped for all his activities. On the opposite page you can see him in his brown tweed shooting outfit. The jacket is buttoned high to the neck, as this is now becoming fashionable, and he wears leather gaiters. A low bowler hat completes his outfit.

Other items from his wardrobe are included in the picture. One of these is a top frock coat for outdoor wear.

The 'Muller-cut-down' hat is interesting. It was a popular hat of the time and named after the murderer, Muller, whose hat led to his identification.

helmet hat

straw hat

'Muller-cut-down' hat

top frock coat

gaiters

waistcoats

The Housekeeper, c. 1872

Here you can see the housekeeper who is the controller of the 250 servants and all the supplies in the squire's house. She is an elderly lady and has worked for the squire's family for many years.

She wears a plain, grey, thick woollen dress, with a cream shawl around her shoulders. Usually, she would wear a white apron but, at present, she has discarded it because she is off-duty in her private sitting room. Although her white lacy cap is out of date it seems to lend her a kind of dignity. She has a chatelaine dangling from her waistband. This is simply a set of short chains on which she carries the keys to all the store cupboards. It is a symbol of her office.

You can imagine that a young girl going to the squire's mansion for an interview as a chambermaid might feel a little intimidated at the thought of being interviewed by this rather formidable lady!

A Footman and a Page Boy, c. 1872

On the right you can see the footman and the page, who are dressed in livery. Livery was a kind of uniform which was provided by wealthy and noble persons for their servants. It was a custom that dated from mediaeval times, the livery colours denoting the household to which the servants belonged. The livery colours of old families were fixed by tradition and the squire's family colour is dark blue.

The footman wears an outfit similar to the evening suit of a gentleman – he even has a white bow tie – but the major difference is that his coat has decorative buttons which are plated with the family crest. His waistcoat has horizontal stripes as he is an indoor footman; the stripes would be vertical if he worked out of doors.

The page has the status of an upper servant and has a quite distinctive uniform. His jacket is short to the waist and closed all down the front so that no waistcoat is worn. He has three rows of buttons arranged on his chest so he is often called 'Buttons'. His outfit is dark blue and his trousers have a red stripe down the side. He is only 14 years old.

Two Maids, c. 1872

On the right you can see one of the housemaids. She is wearing a blue print cotton dress and a blue and lilac print cotton apron. She has a smart cotton cap with streamers, and her hair is carefully pinned up underneath it. You might notice the hint of a bustle at the back of her dress. Although the maids are forbidden to wear 'fashionable' clothes, some of them try to achieve a more fashionable look. Sometimes they resort to wearing old dusters or even newspapers underneath their skirts if they cannot afford a bustle! In the afternoons the housemaid is sometimes required to serve tea and for this she always changes into a black dress. At the moment, the maid is helping the cook by polishing some of the vast collection of copper jelly moulds in the kitchen.

The little scullery maid is only 12 years old and is new to her job. She spends her day scrubbing, washing mountains of dishes and fetching and carrying heavy pots and pans. She is wearing a linen dress of dark green and a bibless apron. She has only a small cap and her curly hair keeps escaping from it while she works. She has been reprimanded for this on a number of occasions by the cook.

The Cook, c. 1872

The cook wears a striped dress and a white, bibbed apron. Her small cap and smart high collar with a bow give her a dignified appearance. Many cooks in lesser establishments would not be as neat and would often wear a neckerchief as a kind of a sweat rag in the hot kitchen atmosphere.

The cook is in charge of the large kitchen and has a number of staff working under her. She is quite strict, but not too harsh as she has been with the family for many years and remembers how she started a long time ago as a little scullery maid. In fact, when the cook was hired it was still the custom for domestic servants to go to the annual 'Mop Fair' in order to be hired. The would-be employees would stand in line, wearing something which would denote their particular 'station'. For example, a cook would wear a red ribbon and carry a basting ladle, while a housemaid would wear a blue ribbon and carry a broom. How do you think it would feel to have to present yourself in this fashion? Do you think it is better to try and obtain a job in the manner in which we go about it today?

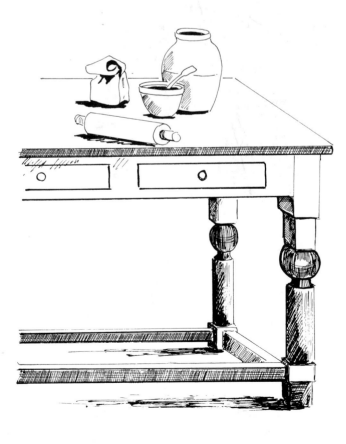

A Gamekeeper and His Wife, c. 1872

This is John, the squire's young gamekeeper. His clothes are both durable and practical for his life out of doors. John's trousers and waistcoat are made of corduroy, a material which was becoming increasingly popular, and his outer coat is made of moleskin, which is a kind of heavy linen. His scarf is worn for warmth in the winter and as a sweat rag in the summer. He also wears a helmet hat and heavy boots. His trousers are hitched up at the knee with a leather strap to help to protect them from wet and mud, but also to stop field mice running up the trouser legs! This strap was called a 'yark', 'york', 'bo-yank', 'liger' or 'pitsea', according to which area of the country you lived in.

This is Elizabeth, the gamekeeper's wife. She is wearing a dark green cotton dress, the skirt of which is hitched up at the back revealing the shorter underskirt below. This is obviously practical because it means that her dress does not get muddy or dirty whilst she is fetching water. In fact, many country women often removed their gowns altogether when working in the fields. For example, it was not unusual to see them helping with harvesting wearing only their petticoats and cotton shifts.

Elizabeth is also wearing a white apron and a sunbonnet. These bonnets were very common as the wide front brim protected the face from sunburn, something which every woman wished to avoid at all costs. (This is, of course, quite unlike our attitude today, when a bronzed and healthy look is considered highly desirable!) The deep frill at the back of the bonnet prevented the wearer from getting sunstroke.

Even in the cities it was common to have no running water and in the country the water from wells and rivers was often muddy and foul-smelling.

A Poacher and His Wife, c. 1872

Here is Arthur, the father of Alice, the little kitchen maid. He used to work on the squire's estate but he lost his job and has taken to poaching in a desperate attempt to provide for his wife and six children.

It would be disastrous if he were caught, as the squire would probably dismiss Alice from her position and Arthur's family would lose even more of its income. Arthur is wearing an old checked woollen coat which has vast pockets, large enough for him to quickly hide any catch that he might make. His waistcoat and scarf are also made of wool and his trousers are corduroy. His trousers are tied at the knee with string rather than a proper strap. A felt hat and strong shoes help to keep him warm whilst he is in the fields.

Arthur's wife cannot afford to be pretty and fashionable like Emma, the squire's new bride. There are no bustles, frills, flounces or satin slippers for her. Instead, she wears a cotton print bodice which is torn in several places, revealing her chemise beneath. Her skirt is also cotton and over it she wears a white apron. Underneath the skirt are several plain petticoats and on her feet a worn pair of boots.

She has no bonnet and her sleeves are rolled up, which means that her face and arms are exposed to the sun so that she will not be able to avoid an unfashionable suntan.

She has been doing laundry for several of her neighbours to try and earn a little extra money for her family.

The Poacher's Children, c. 1872

Here are four of the poacher's children. The older ones do not go to
school, even though an Education Act was passed in 1870 making it
compulsory for all children to attend. This is because Arthur cannot
afford to give all his children the pennies for their school slate and
pencil and, in addition, he needs his older children either to work in the
fields for a little extra money or to help around the house. The
authorities would fine Arthur if they knew he kept his children
from school, but the fines would not be as much as the little
extra money that the children can earn.

Joe is wearing an old felt hat, a scarf, a corduroy coat,
linen trousers and boots. He has the legs of his
trousers rolled up because they are too big for him.

His little sister, Becky, has on an old sunbonnet, and
a neckerchief and wears a pinafore over her
shabby cotton dress. She, too, wears leather
boots. They have very few clothes and in
winter their mother often rubs lard into their
skin to keep them warm and then they do
not remove their clothes for months.

Joe and Becky are taking some
lunch to their eldest brother,
Thomas, who is working for
one of the shepherds on the
squire's estate. In the
meantime, Ellen, who is ten,
is at home in their cottage
looking after the baby. She
wears a pinafore over her
plain cotton dress and lace-
up boots and her hair is left
loose and untidy.

The baby has nothing on his head, even though it is not very warm inside the cottage, and he is wearing a cotton print dress. It was only the poor children who were put into cotton print at birth; the babies of the rich were dressed in beautiful white muslin or lawn.

Now that Ellen's elder sister works in the squire's house and her mother is often out collecting or delivering laundry, Ellen is often given the responsibility of looking after her younger brothers and sisters. Sometimes she has to prepare a meal for the family and help to keep the house clean. What, do you think, would be the dangers of giving a child of ten so much responsibility?

You might like to compare this scene with that depicting Emma and her new baby on page 52.

A Shepherd Boy, c. 1872

Here is 12-year-old Thomas, who is working for a shepherd. The shepherd has kindly loaned a smock to Thomas to help to keep him warm.

Smocks were worn by many agricultural labourers in the nineteenth century as they were so practical. They were usually made of some eight yards of heavy white linen and, therefore, stood away from the body when worn, which meant that they shed the rain during a downpour. They were also windproof and ideal for shepherds, who were exposed to all weathers, though they were often avoided by those working with machinery as they tended to get in the way.

Thomas's smock has a cape collar which he can put up to help shield him from the wind.

Labourers took a great pride in their smocks and often wore them outside working hours. Traditionally, smocks were embroidered with beautiful and elaborate designs, the style varying from county to county.

In his novel *Under the Greenwood Tree* Thomas Hardy describes some countrymen assembling for choir practice and writes that they wore:

. . . snowy white smock frocks embroidered upon their shoulders
and breasts in ornamental forms of hearts, daggers, zigzags . . .

You can see an example of the fine, elaborate embroidery on the smock pictured here.

A Baby in the Family, c. 1873

The first photographs were produced in England in the 1830s, and by the 1870s photography had become very popular amongst the well-to-do. Emma has now had a baby, and the proud squire has had a photograph taken of her and their tiny son.

The baby is wearing a long white muslin gown and for his christening a special gown has been made. It is also of muslin and has been elaborately embroidered with satin stitch. It will be displayed with great pride and will probably be kept in the family and used in future generations. The skirts of both these gowns are over one yard in length, for it was believed that the excess material would help to keep the baby's feet warm and also give the mother or nurse something to hold on to and stop the infant slipping from their arms! (The first pram in which a baby could lie down did not appear in England until the 1870s.)

A baby's first shirt was always open in the front; later he would wear a closed shirt as in the picture. Babies, like their mothers, were burdened with numerous petticoats and were even put into stays when they were about two or three years old. Until the 1850s they always wore caps indoors and out, but by the time Emma had her baby it was generally felt that caps were not necessary indoor wear.

These clothes may look very charming, but can you think of any serious disadvantages they might have had?

christening gown

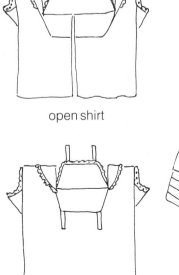

open shirt

petticoat

bonnet

stays

knitted coat

closed shirt

A Glimpse at Fashion, c. 1884

It is the autumn of 1884, and Emma's young niece, Beth, has come from London to stay with the squire's family. She is dressed in the very latest London fashions, which she is proud to show off to her aunt.

Her high-necked dress is cut in the 'princess' style, which means that it has no seam at the waist. It has a waistcoat front of spotted woollen muslin, which is joined to the dress material with strips at the chest and skirt. The muslin is drawn backwards and draped over a very broad bustle. She is also wearing a highly decorative hat, long gloves and bracelets.

Underneath her dress she is wearing an underskirt with a tied-on white cotton bustle, which can be expanded by means of strings.

leather travelling bag

54

The fashions at this time were not very flattering. For example, some women were wearing enormous bustles which distorted their shape to such an extent that they gave the appearance of a protruding shelf, large enough, it was said, to rest a tea tray on! There was also a passion for decorating dresses with real and imitation dead animals. In fact, one magazine of 1884 asked whether cats, dogs and mice were really suitable dress trimmings!

Below you can see a few other items from Beth's wardrobe.

At about this time there was also a fashion for wearing mourning clothes for some considerable period after there had been a death in the family. This fashion had, of course, been started by the Queen herself, who had gone into virtual seclusion after the death of Prince Albert in 1861. Now every draper's shop of any size had a mourning department and there was quite a good business to be had dealing in black crepe. There were even 'degrees' of mourning. For example, a lady would wear a light dress covered with crepe for nine months. After this period she would gradually reduce the layers of crepe, then she would wear a crepe bonnet for six months. After a while she would change to black silk, gradually introducing coloured trimmings and finally re-emerging in ordinary clothing some months later! Many women even wrote to fashion magazines to obtain advice on the exact type of mourning clothes they should be wearing for a particular relative. Pictured here, you can see a crepe bonnet from Beth's wardrobe that she wore when in mourning for her father.

hat with feathers

brown kid and white satin shoes

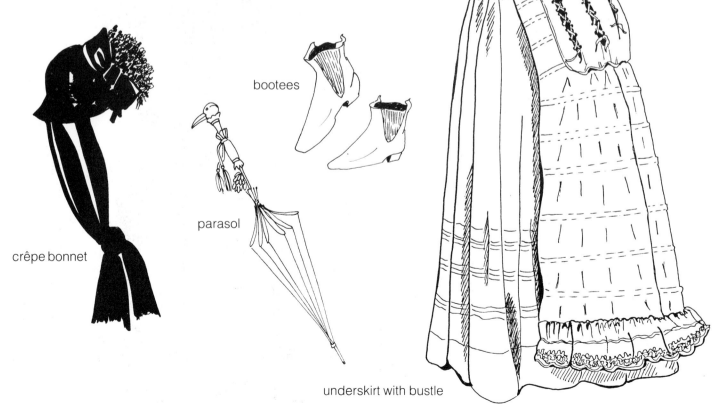

crêpe bonnet

parasol

bootees

underskirt with bustle

Sports Clothes, c. 1894

By 1894, many more women were taking part in sporting activities and their clothes had to be adapted accordingly. The 1890s saw the formation of the Original Lady's Cricketers' Club (1890) and the Ladies Golf Union (1893), and the first international hockey match for ladies (1897). However, one of the most popular sporting activities was bicycling, and here we can see Isabella, one of Emma's children, in her bicycling costume.

Her jacket is double-breasted and has large leg-of-mutton sleeves. Underneath, she is wearing a shirt blouse with a stiffened collar and a man's tie. She also has on wide knickerbockers, coloured stockings made of cotton and a straw hat with stand-up trimmings and a face veil.

Isabella is also fond of tennis, and for this she wears a blouse and a short skirt (two inches off the ground!), a cap, a tie and gloves. Like many Victorian women, she also enjoys the occasional trip to the seaside and a dip in the sea. Opposite, you can see one of her bathing costumes which is made of cotton with insets of embroidery.

These outfits may appear very cumbersome to us, and it is difficult to imagine participating in sport hampered by so much material. However, we must remember that these clothes were quite revolutionary in their time and were frowned upon by many as being quite scandalous. You might like to think about how frequently sports clothes eventually become everyday wear. For example, today, it is quite acceptable for people to walk about the streets in track suits, tennis shoes, shorts and the type of garments that used to be reserved for sporting events. Why do you think this happens?

At this time, women were beginning their struggle for emancipation and it is interesting that their desire to be on an equal footing with men is reflected in the clothes that they wore. For example, the wide, leg-of-mutton sleeves gave ladies a masculine, rather aggressive appearance rather than emphasizing their femininity. What other features of these clothes appear to you to give Isabella a masculine rather than a feminine look?

A Day at the Races, c. 1894

Here is Isabella at the races in 1894. She is dressed in a spotted taffeta dress which, once again, has very wide sleeves. You can see that her tiny waist has been emphasized, giving her an hourglass shape. She wears a wide-brimmed hat of straw, trimmed with ostrich feathers, and elbow-length gloves with bracelets over the top.

Even though Victorian women were beginning to move towards greater freedom in their sports clothes you will notice from the lace, frills and fancy trimmings on this dress that they had a long way to go before they could experience the freedom of movement in their everyday wear which we enjoy today.

Isabella is being escorted by the young gentleman whom she is going to marry. He is the son of a rich landowner and is dressed in the height of fashion.

He is wearing a high-buttoned frock coat with a small collar. His shirt collar and front are starched and he wears a bow tie. His striped trousers have no crease and he has a black silk top hat and fawn kid gloves and, of course, he is carrying a cane. His hair is fashionably short. In fact, if men wore their hair long at this time they were frowned upon and condemned as poets or musicians. (The Victorian poet Tennyson wore his hair long.)

And so we leave the solicitor's grandchildren to enjoy the races. You might be interested to compare their clothes with those worn by their grandparents on Derby Day in 1858, which you will see over the page. What changes have taken place over the years?

Conclusion

We have seen, through the characters in this book, not only how the fashions changed during the nineteenth century, but also how a person's style of dress can tell us a great deal about his or her profession and lifestyle. For example, the rich man who paraded his wealth by providing his wife and daughters with expensive frills and finery contrasted with the poor man who thought little of fashion but, instead, used clothing merely as a practical way of keeping warm.

You might like to think carefully about the gulf between the rich and the poor in Victorian times and the difference in their clothing. Do you think, for example, that a rich lady in her petticoats, corset and crinoline cage was more comfortable than a poor woman dressed in her practical though unfashionable clothes? The poor women's clothes may have been dirty, but how hygienic were the long trains on the dresses of the rich ladies that trailed in the mud and filth in the streets and could not be washed or dry cleaned? Was a rich baby, smothered in material and lace, any happier than a poor family's baby, whose clothes at least gave him room to grow and breathe?

We have seen also how styles of dress often reflect changes in society. For example, the sombre, rather drab colours of men's clothing reflected the grey, smoky atmosphere of the industrial cities, and the leg-of-mutton sleeves and sports clothes of the ladies of the 1890s signalled the beginning of women's search for equality. Can you think of any other examples like this?

Derby Day, 1858

Queen Victoria's reign was a long one and saw many changes. There were technical developments, which revolutionized industry, a vast improvement in communication services, which allowed a greater movement of goods and people, and a gradual swing towards a greater freedom in fashions. Towards the end of the reign there was a sense that fashions were beginning to 'let go' as the Queen, herself sombre and dignified to the last, neared the end of her long life. During the course of your studies perhaps you could examine the relationship between the changing shape of Victorian society and the fascinating, ever-changing shape of fashion.

vagrants, 1858

Glossary

bustle	a pad, originally made of horsehair and later of wire, that was tied around a lady's waist under her dress in order to make the dress stand out at the back *(pages 37 and 55)*
cambric	a very fine linen fabric *(page 12)*
cashmere	a fine, soft wool *(page 10)*
chatelaine	a set of short chains attached to a lady's belt and used for carrying keys *(page 40)*
chemise	a woman's undergarment, usually made of soft cotton material and worn underneath the stays *(page 11)*
crinolette	a half crinoline which gave fullness to the back of the skirt *(page 37)*
crinoline	sometimes called a crinoline cage; a hooped petticoat made of flexible steel or whalebone and worn in order to support the wide skirts fashionable in the middle of Victoria's reign *(pages 24-7)*
gaiters	a covering of stiff fabric or leather for wearing below the knee as a protection against wet and mud, etc. *(page 39)*
livery	a uniform provided by wealthy persons for their servants *(page 41)*
mantle	a lady's loose cloak *(page 25)*
Muller-cut-down	a short top hat popular in the early 1870s and named after the murderer Muller *(page 38)*
muslin	a delicately woven cotton fabric *(page 54)*
pantalettes	long drawers, worn by women and children, extending to just below the calf and usually embroidered with lace trimmings *(page 13)*
porter's knot	a pad worn by porters to support goods carried on the head *(page 29)*
princess style	a dress that is cut all in one – that is, with no seam at the waist *(page 54)*
smock	a garment made of heavy linen and usually beautifully embroidered; worn by agricultural workers *(page 50)*
stays	a corset, stiffened with whalebone and fastened with lacing *(pages 11 and 53)*
yark	(also called a 'york', 'bo-yank', 'liger' or 'pitsea'); a leather strap used to hitch up men's trousers just below the knee *(page 46)*

Places to Visit

Here are a few ideas for some interesting places to visit which would help you in your study of Victorian life and costume.

Bath Museum of Costume, Assembly Rooms, Bath, Avon.

Bethnal Green Museum of Childhood (a branch of the Victoria and Albert Museum).

Gallery of English Costume, Platt Hall, Platt Fields, Rusholme, Manchester M14 5LL

Geffrye Museum, Kingsland Road, Shoreditch, London E2 8EA.

Hitchin Museum and Art Gallery, Hitchin, Herts.

Museum of London, London Wall, London EC2Y 5HN.

National Portrait Gallery, St Martin's Place, Trafalgar Square, London WC2H 0HE.

Tate Gallery, Millbank, London SW1P 4RG.

Victoria and Albert Museum, Cromwell Road, South Kensington, London SW7 2RL.

Book List

Adams, Carol — *Ordinary Lives One Hundred Years Ago*, Virago, 1982

Allen, Eleanor — *Victorian Children*, Black, 1973

Black, J.A. & Garland, M. — *A History of Fashion*, 2nd ed., Orbis Publishing, 1980

Bradfield, Nancy — *Costume in Detail, 1730-1930*, Harrap, 1968

Bradfield, Nancy — *Historical Costumes of England, 1066-1956*, Harrap, 1958

Brook, Iris — *English Costume of the 19th Century*, Black, 1929

Barthorp, Michael — *British Infantry Uniforms since 1660*, Blandford Books, 1982

Braun-Rondsdorf, Margarete — *The Wheel of Fashion*, Thames & Hudson, 1964

Cassin-Scott, Jack — *Costume and Fashion in Colour, 1760-1920*, Blandford, 1971

Cassin-Scott, Jack — *Costumes and Settings for Historical Plays, Volume 5: The Nineteenth Century*, Batsford, 1980

Cumming, Valerie — *Exploring Costume History, 1500-1900*, Batsford, 1981

Cunnington, C.W. & P. — *Handbook of English Costume in the 19th Century*, 2nd ed., Faber, 1966

Cunnington, C.W. & P. — *History of Underclothes*, revised ed., Faber, 1981

Cunnington, C.W. & Lucas, C. — *Occupational Costume in England*, Black, 1967

Cunnington, P. & Buck, A. — *Children's Costume in England*, 1300-1900, Black, 1965

Cunnington, Phillis — *Nineteenth-Century Costumes*, Faber, 1970

Daulte, Francois Renoir — *Les Impressionnistes*, Diffusion Princesse, Paris, 1974

Dorner, Jane — *Fashion*, Octopus Books, 1974

Evans, Hilary & Mary — *The Victorians: At Home and At Work*, David & Charles, 1973

Ewing, E. — *History of Children's Costume*, Batsford, 1977

Foster, Vanda — *Bags and Purses*, Batsford, 1982

Holland, Vyvyan — *Hand-Coloured Fashion Plates, 1770-1899*, Batsford, 1955

Huxley, Elspeth — *Florence Nightingale*, Weidenfeld & Nicolson, 1975

Laver, James — *Costume and Fashion, a Concise History*, 2nd ed., Thames & Hudson, 1982

Laver, James — *Costume Through the Ages*, Thames & Hudson, 1964

Laver, James — *Fashion & Fashion Plates, 1800-1900*, Penguin, 1942

Laver, James — *Taste & Fashion*, 2nd ed., Harrap, 1945

Lister, Margot — *Costume: An Illustrated Survey*, Herbert Jenkins, 1968

Longmate, N. — *The Workhouse*, Temple Smith, 1974

Matyjaszkiewicz, Krystyna (ed.) — *James Tissot*, Phaidon Press, 1984

Mayhew, Henry — *London Labour and the London Poor*, Frank Cass, 1967

Mayo, Janet, — *A History of Ecclesiastical Dress*, Batsford, 1984

Priestley, J.B. — *Victoria's Heyday*, Heinemann, 1972

Quennell, Peter — *The Day before Yesterday*, Dent, 1978

Sichel, Marion — *Costume Reference, Volume 6: The Victorians*, Batsford, 1978

Speed, P.F. — *Learning and Teaching in Victorian Times*, 2nd ed., Longman, 1983

Squire, Geoffrey — *Dress, Art and Society, 1560-1970*, Studio Vista, 1974

Victoria and Albert Museum — *400 Years of Fashion*, 1984

Williams-Mitchell, Christobel — *Dressed for the Job*, Blandford Books, 1982

Winter, Gordon — *A Country Camera, 1844-1914*, Penguin, 1966

Wood, Christopher — *Victorian Panorama: Paintings of Victorian Life*, Faber, 1976

Children's Fashion's of the Nineteenth Century, (Introduction and notes by James Laver) Batsford, 1951

Ladies Companion and Monthly Magazine, Vol. IV, Rogerson & Co., 1857

Victorian Life in Photographs (Introduction by William Sanson), Thames & Hudson, 1974.

Things to Do

1. Visit your local museum and find out if they have any examples of Victorian costume or items from Victorian homes for you to look at.
2. Try making some Victorian costumes with your friends and then act out a scene together using some of the characters from this book.
3. The sewing machine was one invention that influenced fashion and the clothing industry. Try to find out more about other machines involved in the making of clothes. For example, the machines used in a cotton factory.
4. Find out more about tailors and dressmakers and the working conditions of those who made the fine garments worn by the rich.
5. Find some books on army uniforms and make some drawings of different soldiers who fought in the Crimean War.
6. Look at the life of Florence Nightingale in more detail. Find out how she influenced the nursing profession and make some drawings of different nurses uniforms. Investigate the working conditions of nurses both before and after Florence Nightingale.
7. Have a look at Charlotte Bronte's novel, *Jane Eyre*. What kind of clothes did children wear in a Victorian children's home? Compare the clothes worn by a governess and those worn by wealthy women.
8. Look at Victorian servants in detail. Make some sketches of different costumes that might have been worn by servants working in a large country house.
9. The railways enabled many people to take trips to the seaside. Find out what they used to wear on the beach. Compare this with the garments we wear today when sunbathing. Do a short project on the history of the swimming costume.
10. How do you think better communications affected fashion in Victorian times?
11. Find out more about your family history. Which of your relatives lived in Victorian times? What kind of clothes did they wear and what did they do for a living?

c. 1898